Solitary Confinement

Isaiah Chung

BookLeaf
Publishing

Presentation by *BookLeaf Publishing*

Web: www.bookleafpub.com

E-mail: info@bookleafpub.com

ISBN: 9789357618878

First edition 2023

DEDICATION

For my brother, Jeremiah.

ACKNOWLEDGEMENT

To Professor Orr. Thank you for putting up with me.

PREFACE

My roommate moved out after the first semester of college. Whether it was because of me, or his external circumstances, we will never know. However, this suddenly empty room allowed for a quiet atmosphere, an environment I had never really been in before. This book is the product of thinking out loud.

some Times

i suppose, at some
Times i feel as if i throw myself,
Smooth back my hair and features as the
spotlight hits
My face,
to Be something i am not.

They call that a people pleaser, a term
describing the lengths one goes to support the
people near them,
But for me, pleasing people could be,

i suppose,

Synonymous to a cry for help,
where some
Times
at night i fold my cranes
and wish as if they came to life,
Assuring me of my intrinsic worth and that i am
Not
just another Face in the Crowd.

And some
Times
this desperation becomes sooted - cracked with
this primal
need to be held, and to Hold

The papers i scour through scream and shout and
blare and howl
Demanding looks, reads, attention,

pitiful, really.

claiming, chanting, chorusing, "These are some
Times We're Going Through!"

and I couldn't agree more.

On Being Stoic

"Things that are within your control: your thoughts and actions. Things that are outside your control: everything else" - The Stoicism belief of the Dichotomy of Control.

Thoughts are powerful. And almost always, thought leads to action. Our individualistic nature allows us to be the captain of our ship, the pioneer of our future.

And yet, we desire a sense of community. To know that others share our belief, our nature, our thoughts. Some of the earliest communities banded together for needed survival; strength in numbers. Community is important, in that when we ever feel alone, we can ameliorate the loneliness through a group effort.

But community should not be sought as a priority. Sometimes, being alone is the more important action to do, to drown in your thoughts, and to relive the past - director's cut of course. I still wallow through regret and poignant what-if's my whole life. Forget the Butterfly Effect, I am a mere Caterpillar.

Pattered batches and battered patches. I inadvertently tried to be a jack-of-all-trades at one point my whole life. Cooking, chess, piano, running. But as soon as I chased those, more tantalizing and excitingly-new prospects came along, resulting in leaving them behind to pursue the unknown. Who knows why.

Maybe for my sense of self, maybe for crossing off a checklist of to-dos, maybe for college even.

I wonder with my current interests and loves, if I will leave them behind one day, chasing after a bigger-and-better.

And I worry again, sinking far beneath the surface, even deeper than the buried bones of my grandparents, into the crevices and still unreached parts of my brain, scouring for meaning, even if I know I'm looking in the wrong place.

Will I be who I want to be? Or is that just a misconception?

We let our emotions get the best of us, when life doesn't go the way we precisely, down to the dot, want it to. And I realize this, and still I err on the wrong side knowing of my sins and yet unable to stop myself from stopping.

And slowing. Oh, the world moves so slow sometimes that I become restless and anxious, letting fear grab my ribcage and split me down the middle. And I feel cheated.

I AM SUPPOSED TO BE THE CAPTAIN OF MY BOAT. I AM SUPPOSED TO BE THE PIONEER OF MY FUTURE.

If so, then why don't I feel in control?

stimuli

5

your peace
and claims of unity
is a veneer of shattered glass, too small even to
glitter in the moonlight

and as i sit on these cold stone steps
watching the group trundle up
even they too are not used to such sight

or blindness, rather.

and it is all ruined,
all brought to naught,
a lesson of Munich if and when you shatter the
glass further

to microscopic grains of agony,
something i was promised,
a future not crumbled, not folded, not ripped, but
diluted,

maybe i am too sad to weep,
or too happy to laugh,
these emotions are the same, after all,
stimuli.

and when i see happiness,
it fills me with a rage so intense and dark,
an anger larger than myself,
expanding,
to the point where i fear the deflation more than
the pop,
because that means it's still there,
rather than lost to the atmosphere

and nothing,
not friends, not scores, not even scripture,
can currently or unconditionally take this away
from me,
because it is my identity.

and sometimes i yearn to be unfeeling,
to not experience the end of good things,
to not be filled with a sadness of the instance
happening once and only once

and i want to erase and begone.

Good Enough

Opaque tubules, choking each precious
white-hot breath,
A far-too-thin frame, bony arms, hurting feet,
Slanted uneven eyes, complementing an equally
uneven backbone,
Yellow skin.

And,
Knowing what happens to people like me
Knowing what happens to those who begin
broken and battered,
Knowing what happens when the climb becomes
Sisyphean,

instead of saying, "It is good.", God said, "Good
enough."

And I sit, slumped, shocked at my existence,
Curious if my fractional intrinsicity yields
fractional results
Lost and disorientated, but certain on one truth:

I don't ever want to hear the words, "Good
enough." again.

Heat

The cells cry out in anguish,
Heat: Sun-kissed becomes Sun-Tzu,
Imagining the polar landscape of the
South Pole does nothing for the slowly-tanning
skin,

Horchata,
Evian,
A variety of the sinful, impossible, forbidden
even,
Taken from my blackened hands, cracked with
the unbearable temperature

Calculations become muddled as thoughts of
Ameliorating this burning sensation in the back
of my throat and
Nape increases, an exponential function stopped
by no carrying capacity

Freedom of speech and other
Unalienable rights slowly pale in
Comparison to
Knowing that there is no freedom to slake thirst.

I cannot process
Thinking, even, despite melting in a pile of
bubbling
Skin, bone, marrow, completed with two
Eyes on top? Or inside?
Lost in translation as my mouth
Freezes, despite the fires all around me.

and the word 'love'

and the word 'love'

shouldn't be flaunted around,
as if it were something common,

because love isn't common.

'love' should be whispered,
the maraschino on top
after a long stroll through the forest, hands
enclasped, eyes drifting everywhere and
anywhere except for where it should be.

'love' should be kept in a small box,
held close to the sapphire blood lub-dubbing
away,
desperately, or it diffuses into the white void

and it is hate, not apathy,
for 'love' can tip the scales, ever so slightly,
to change an opposite into just a posit.

and when I see her,
black hair, soft smile, the gentleness that abates
the brusqueness of the Outside,

in a voice so soft it can be heard by only me and
the dryads,
I crumple my fingers in a fit of agonizing
Purgatory,

"I want to love you."

Bonsai Trees Along the Road

Why is it that I feel pity when I pass the
Man on the side of the road, selling bonsai trees,

Perhaps it is that I jump to conclusion, and
assume that he has nothing better to do.
Perhaps it is all he can do
Perhaps it is fate.

I don't want to look, and yet I do.

And my soul claws its way out of my head,
Spins lazily in the air, and with its
Soft, dark aura fixates me into place,
And suddenly I am him.

Long trays with carefully ornate pots,
With a small, delicate tree almost clumsily
potted, the grafts
Pinpointed, stretching towards the infinite
parade of vehicles passing by,
An audience of nothing but the sycamores,
But even they dare not watch, jealous of their
smaller counterparts

Lowering the Activation Energy

The 5 stages of a relationship is as follows:

1: The Honeymoon Phase
2: Doubting and Questioning
3: Rumination
4: Plateau
5: True Love

I want to jump from 1: to 5:

Without suffering in between

And I have come to the conclusion that it's
impossible
Without my catalyst.

Molecules

The safety of privilege is at first preceded by the
privilege of safety
In which we may have our thoughts to turn to,
To brood in, being our own king or queen
And ruling our thoughts,
Being safe.

Only now is it that I consider, now being outside
of my bubble,
That maybe I shouldn't see my thoughts as a
privilege,
But a misconception of corpuscularianism, a
sick twist of fate,

Or was it of molecules?

Mixed Signals

I've been getting some mixed signals recently from
this girl, and I'm not too sure on what to think.

Do I,
As an aspiring doctor,
With my scalpel, attendees and medical degree
Stitch together the situation,
Callusing both my heart and bleeding fingers,
Ready to assure if the worst occurs,
And to steel my heart if the best happens?

Do I,
As a shaky and insecure Christian,
Pray to a God I have doubted my whole life,
Hoping that the universe or some other deity,
Grants me a wish, to maybe,
Hold her hand,
Brush her hair,
Whisper bitter inevitable nothings into her ears,
At maybe the cost of my arms or some other
mythological fee?

Do I,
As a college student,
Ruminate with my peers,
Spending time in a small university to solve a small
problem,
Knowing that this memory will etch its place in my
life's chapter
Instead of, perhaps, something more worthwhile?

Do I,
As a human being,
Knowing of my negligible stature compared to the
universe, its history, its vastness
Consider myself a pawn in this game of Life,
Knowing what will be, will be?

Or do I,
Jump out of my identity for a split second,
And ask her?

Baggage

17

When I inevitably leave this Earth,
I don't want to carry any baggage with me
In the terminal separating this lowly land to the great sky,

It would be rather difficult, I suppose,
To dispose of some of the most precious things to me,
But can I truly ever be reborn if I start with a precursor?

Wednesdays

I am the happiest on Fridays, and the saddest on
Mondays,
And the most broken on Wednesdays, because
I should talk to that girl in my class and
Strike some conversation
Or laugh over a good joke with my
Friends to remind myself of our fraternal existence

But I can't,
Even when the hours slowly transition from muddy to
glimmering,
I can't force myself to be something I'm not.
Not anymore, at least.

And as such, I cannot metamorphosize,
And as such, I am left behind,

In which the time leaves me to fetally curl next to my
thoughts,
And my depression.

Flatline

Would it be more tragic to
Not feel, than to experience
The worst pain, horrifying agony?

For me, I am restless,
My hands and brain need to be occupied,
Clamoring to touch and hurt and be hurt,
Since I know that one day,
They will be lifeless.

So yes, it is more tragic, I think,
To not feel,
Because in pain, we still experience tribulation,
Whereas not feeling leaves us at a perpetual
Flatline.

An Ode to Spotify

It is beautiful,
In that I can make a playlist to
Describe some of the more incomprehensible
emotions I feel.

The angst I feel tonight,
Or the grit I experience when jump roping,
The loneliness I feel when I balance buffers in the
lab,

Can be represented by sound, if not by soul.

And when I am the spectator,
Watching those, prostrate, hands up,
Or smiling while drinking thick, muddy coffee,
The tears of those with broken hearts,

Their experiences
If not lives,
can be fronted by sound, if not by soul.

There is an Inuit word, called
Iktsuarpok,
Which describes the frustration of waiting for another
to arrive,

Where is
My playlist?

Degrees of Freedom

I fall in love easily,
Not because of the hormones, governed by my
pituitary gland, dictating how I should live my
life.

…well, maybe to a degree.

But also of my acknowledgment
That the world, time, life,
Is fleeting, and every moment is but a snapshot
in an infinite lockbox.

And as I fall, forever,
Until I hit the ground,
I want to have someone with me,
Falling with me,

Assuring me that it is not only I that
continuously falls into this void I treasure more
than anything else,
And with soft hands intertwined,
Clasping our hearts together,
Understanding that our eyes are not windows to
our souls, but a window to something greater,
Something more.
A dance of souls.

Mamihlapinatapai,
A succinct Yaghan word describing shared
interest between two parties, but hesitation to
initiate action,
Is called into question here.

And Won,
The Korean word describing the unwillingness
to accept reality
And to defer from the illusion,
Tells me that I am desperate for a fantasy.

Do I love because I care for the other,
Or because I am afraid to love?

What pushes me on

My anxiety gets the better of me sometimes,

I wish that I could be my ideal self if not for
worrying if I am

Pretentious, like my writing,
Self-righteous, like my morals,
Harsh and judgmental, like the shaping of my
identity,
Shocking and sickening, like my personality.

Worrying too much might be detrimental, but at
least it's motivating for now.

On Marijuana

To be swept away by green clouds
And embraced into an indelible lethargy,
Slurred words, contentment,
Is ignorance really bliss,
If weed is a pathway there?

Slivers of Myself

25

Suppose there is an arbitrary circle,
And this circle represents 'attention'
Or 'love', or 'focus', or whatever sacrifice one
human must make for another,

I am happy, because that circle is mine.
And when another is introduced into that circle,
My 'whole' becomes a 'fraction',
And I feel jealous, sad,
Disappointed at the prospect in which
I cannot possess the 'whole'

If I had no experience,
If there were no competitors,
So that my 'whole' would always be my
'whole',
Would I be happy?
Knowing that I am at the top?

I roll down, to a 'sliver' of myself,
And know that I will never be 'whole' again,
Since others are present.

PageFlips

I can feel it.

My chapter is ending, and moving into a new
one,
And maybe I'm slightly conservative,
I don't want to see my routines and habits
change into something new,
Because to me,
The unknown scares me.

I find it more comfortable to replay the 'easy
mode' instead of moving onto more difficult
levels,
But I recognize that I have to grow too,
Even if I want to stay a child forever.

Angst&Being

I suppose one of my bigger fears, aside from
being lonely,
Is being too intimidating.

Since there's that balance of having control and
giving it.

I overthink on my friendships too much,
To which the slightest dissonance makes me
question my own validity,
And whether or not I should be detracting from
their potential happiness,
Souring it with my gloominess

Combine that with a hint of impostor syndrome,
And when I get support and reassurance of my
worth,
I doubt that, believing myself to not be worthy
of these accolades

It's also impossible to discuss this issue with my
friends
Or should I even call them that? Friends?
Humans?

Since they see me as confident, happy-go-lucky,
social,
When sometimes,
I feel lonely despite my 'network'

One of the worst feelings in the world would
Probably be

Feeling

They say that anxiety makes the result
A hundred,
No, a thousand times worse,

But what happens when my problem is my
anxiety?

Setting the kindle aflame with thoughts of
imperfection and anguish
Twists my heart into a disheveled knot,
And further and further the distortion appears,
To which a sob of despair is the only intangible
sequence holding my worthlessness back,

Reminding me that I am human,
I feel,
And sometimes, I am imperfect,
Even if I don't want to be.

I compare myself to others in a better state than
me,
Cursing my procrastination and lethargy,
Cursing why my life is not as copacetic,
My coping mechanisms, however, are not
ascetic

And I recognize that.
And it still hurts, but
Is an infinitely better feeling than feeling
nothing at all.

You feel?